Scenes

for Teens, by Teens

Diane Christiansen

iUniverse, Inc.

New York   Bloomington

Scenes for Teens, by Teens
A collection by Diane Christiansen

iUniverse books may be ordered through booksellers or by contacting:

iUniverse
1663 Liberty Drive
Bloomington, IN 47403
www.iuniverse.com
1-800-Authors (1-800-288-4677)

Because of the dynamic nature of the Internet, any Web addresses or links
contained in this book may have changed since publication and may no longer be
valid. The views expressed in this work are solely those of the author and do not
necessarily reflect the views of the publisher, and the publisher hereby disclaims
any responsibility for them.

ISBN: 978-1-4502-1878-8 (pbk)
ISBN: 978-1-4502-1879-5 (ebook)

Printed in the United States of America

iUniverse rev. date: 5/12/10

"I knew a phoenix in my youth, so let them have their day."

- William Butler Yeats

Table of Contents

* Acknowledgements ix

Scenes for Two Girls

* "TV Talk"   Paige Blatt   3
* "My Tadpole Brother"   Mary Ann Springer   5
* "What About Jordan?"   Tess Christiansen   7
* "My Dad Is…"   Kelly Nish   10
* "Mom Needs a Man"   Paige Blatt   12
* "What Happened to the New Guy"   Mary Ann Springer   14
* "Models and Comedians Don't Mix"   Mary Ann Springer   16
* "The Third Person"   Kelly Nish   18
* "Diet Craze"   Kelly Nish   20
* "Just Friends"   Samantha Grossman   22
* "Guys Don't Listen"   Tess Christiansen   24
* "Saturday Night"   Amber Gonzales   26

Scenes for Two Boys

* "Best Friends"   Tess Christiansen   33
* "Bet on Love"   Tess Christiansen   35

Scenes for a Boy and a Girl

* "At Least I've Got a Date"   Tess Christiansen   41
* "Jacky and Chad"   Monique Almanza   44
* "The Fight"   Chelsea Matthews   46
* "Geeks and Jocks"   Kelly Nish   48
* "Money Rules"   Lee C. Korelitz   50
* "Family TV Talk"   David Phillips   53
* "Tech Support"   David Phillips   57

ACKNOWLEDGEMENTS

I am grateful to a number of talented and visionary individuals for their assistance in completing this book. Because it is a collection of scenes written by my gifted and fabulous teen-aged acting students, I would like to thank them individually by listing their names under the scenes they wrote for this book, please note them by name as you read each scene. Many are working actors here in Hollywood. Each scene represents a chapter of their lives shared so generously with all of us and now to you. I feel this to be sacred work and I hold unconditional love for young actors so willing to reveal so much of themselves so completely. So, to each of them I am endlessly grateful. To the parents and families who provided lessons and drove them to classes and to auditions week after week to further their dreams and their careers. I wanted to thank you for your love, support, commitment to them and to our work. The young actor in Hollywood is not unlike any other teenager in America, with the same issues, the same growth patterns, the same desires and experiences. The only difference is that we hold it up to the light for all to view, on the big screen, the Television, in videos and on stage. This takes such courage. This is truly the path of the artist.

The execution of this book has taken nearly as much time as I spent collecting scenes from students. (Mostly because of our busy lives here in L.A.) However, it finally happened and several key people have contributed so much to its execution. I would especially like to thank my friends and associates who were diligent and thorough.

To the final draft editor, Dianne Tangle-Cate, for your expertise, your talent, time and your clarity. For being not only my friend, but the committed woman that you are, for your timeliness and orderliness, for your talent and your insights. Keeping me on track when both of us had way too many duties , especially as mothers of young actors who have careers that we have nurtured and helped grow. For editing this book as if it was your own, and making me so proud of it. I am indebted to you for life!!

My humble thanks to Emily Ball, whose ideas, creativity and thinking helped see me through during pilot season, to the next level. To your ability to get something produced on time !! You are so wonderful at that, and for producing the showcase which featured these scenes to agents, managers and casting directors in Hollywood and making sure the actors were on target with them. For making sure the language was consistent and real. For helping bridge any gap between adult acceptability and teen endorsement. For driving as far as you did to work in my office on it while simultaneously booking private lessons for me, answering phones and filing. I will always remember your generous spirit and your power of play!!!

My literary Assistant, 16 year old, Maddie McGuire moved to Hollywood from Chicago this year and I was fortunate enough to engage her many many skills as my final Assistant on this project. I will be very lucky to keep her working on the book considering what an exceptional young actress she is. I predict really great things for her in TV & Film. In the meantime, I am the luckiest person alive to have her on my team, driving this book home with iUniverse. She has managed to actually make it happen during my busiest months ever ! For this I will be eternally grateful and can't even imagine not having Maddie on my team for Life !! She is already unbelievable for her age, proving that age is just a number. Her maturity, generosity and over all skills and talent are the reason you are reading and using this wonderful collection today and she is the reason we will have book signings and books distributed. She is the light at the end of the tunnel and I am overwhelmed with endless gratitude to her. Thank you Maddie, for being the miracle this book needed.

Finally, to Jessica Urdank, my gifted friend, student and ultimate book assistant. If it were not for you, this book would not be in existence. To your willingness to do whatever needed to be done quickly and with such an open mind and heart . I am grateful for the pleasure of working with such a great spirit. A woman who will follow through to the end and make sure it winds up in the right hands, on the right bookshelves and in perfect order. To your attention to details, and to your flexible soul. Flowing with every change and whim that inspired me. To a beautiful super model and talented actress who can play all of the characters with ease and grace. I am truly blessed to have met you exactly when I did. I thank God for you !

I especially want to thank the books greatest contributor, my daughter, Tess, who not only wrote most of the scenes in this collection, but who also inspired me to publish it in the first place. I thank you for staying in class for 10 years and never going anywhere else, even when I tired to send you to others. For writing scenes without anyone asking you to. To bringing them in when no one expected it, for opening my eyes to the many facets of the teenagers soul that need full self expression. For opening my eyes to all that teens have to express and for using our acting class to be that platform. For using class to develop into such a talented writer and for using your talent to perform your own scenes. You and your brother, Maximilian, are my greatest gifts and I thank you both for being in my life, my classes and my plays. I must thank Max for sticking around the house while in college and making Tess and I laugh at ourselves and our Diva roller coaster ride. For coming to showcases and for being our in-house artist and stage hand for so many productions!!

I also want to thank Casey Erikson for taking the candid and beautiful photo of Tess for the book cover, at your "Love-in" at Valencia high school in 2006. I believe your future as a photographer is indeed promising!!

Thank you to the many friends, associates, parents and actors who encouraged the production of this book. Whose encouragement I could count on and who were my personal cheerleaders.

Most of all, thanks to my incredible students, who year after year teach me more than I can ever teach them!

<u>Scenes for Two Girls</u>

TV TALK

By Paige Blatt

(Two girls are hanging out in a living room.)

ALEX: Sarah, I'm really having a problem here. I don't know what to do about Blair! I think he doesn't like me anymore and might be starting to like Jessie.

SARAH: No way, you and Blair are totally perfect for each other. Ew, why would he like Jessie more than you? Oh, my gosh! This is totally like Brooke and Peyton! Lucas liked Brooke and they were so cute together, but all of a sudden he was all over Peyton behind her back! *(Gasp.)* Well, that won't happen with you, don't worry, I promise!

ALEX: Hmmm…I don't know. I mean, Blair and Jessie were really close before I ever met him.

SARAH: Whoa, that's true! It's like Ryan and Theresa on *The O.C.* Marrisa and Ryan were going out, but Theresa was always in the picture because of their past. Jessie does have a boyfriend—she and Shane have been together for awhile. *(Gasp.)* BUT… Theresa from *The O.C.* had her boyfriend, Eddie, too!

ALEX: You're right, Jessie does have Shane. I think I'm just getting worked up about nothing.

SARAH: Yeah, but so did Marissa, and now look who's pregnant! I think you need to watch out. First, you're suspicious when you see them eating lunch together. Then, all of a sudden, Blair starts to get busier and busier. Before you know it, you are sitting at their wedding, all alone! This is horrible…we need to do something about this!

ALEX: YOU'RE RIGHT!!! I mean—

SARAH: —This can't be good. I remember in *Head Over Heels,* when Amanda walks in on her boyfriend, doing the you-know-what with that beautiful model, and decides to swear off all men! THAT CAN'T HAPPEN TO YOU! I mean, that's just awful! I can't believe this is happening, Are you OK?

ALEX: Sarah, I think you are going a little far.

SARAH: Wait a second…is Jessie your cousin?

ALEX: NO, Sarah! What does that have to do with anything?

SARAH: Well, in *A Guy's Thing,* remember when Selma Blaine's fiancé decides to leave her for her cousin! I can tell you one thing, I am pretty sure that she didn't see that one coming! Could you? Yeah, that's what I thought. You poor girl, right when things start to get good between you two, he goes behind your back!! Don't worry, I will be here for you, no matter what, even if I have to pull a Tom Cruise and go *Mission Impossible!*

ALEX: Sarah, stop! You're talking nonsense! My life isn't a movie, OK? Now *you* are the one getting too worked up. Everything will be OK. But just in case, we should go rent some Jackie Chan movies or something, because if he really is cheating, we'll need to know how to kick his butt!

MY TADPOLE BROTHER

By Mary Ann Springer

(Two girls are laboring over their homework.)

TRACY: I'm tired of homework.

DANIELA: Yeah, who isn't?

TRACY: We should take an hour break and go somewhere, do something.

DANIELA: We are *not* going to the school to vandalize the property!

TRACY: I wasn't thinking that!

DANIELA: You've thought of it before…why not now?

TRACY: Whatever. Hey, how about we go shopping at the mall?

DANIELA: I am not going to go blow all my money, then feel a rush to get home to complete my homework.

TRACY: Oh, we should go to the beach. We could watch guys play volleyball! You can bring your homework and do it on the beach, where it is *so* nice and relaxing. What do you say?

DANIELA: *(Sarcastically.)* Yeah, that's a great idea, if only we could get there. We can't drive, and your mom isn't home.

TRACY: We could ride our bikes down there. It's not too far.

DANIELA: I don't have a bike.

TRACY: You can borrow my brother's.

DANIELA: *(Sweetly.)* Do you think he'd let me ride his BMX bike?

TRACY: Yeah, sure.

DANIELA: Don't we have to ask him if I can use it?

TRACY: No, he'll be cool with it.

DANIELA: But shouldn't we ask, just in case?

TRACY: You must really want to talk to my brother. *(Gasp.)* You like my brother, don't you!?

DANIELA: No, I…I don't like Zach, I mean, your brother.

TRACY: Oh you do, you do, you do! I can totally tell. *(Shocked.)* Oh my gosh…you like my brother! Ewwww!

DANIELA: OK, maybe I do a little, like a tadpole.

TRACY: A tadpole? Like a baby frog?

DANIELA: OK. How about we go to the beach or go do… something else?

TRACY: OK…anything to help you *not* think about my tadpole brother.

DANIELA: OK, drop it! Let's go!

WHAT ABOUT JORDAN?

By Tess Christiansen

(A girl is lounging, doing her nails, when another girl enters the room.)

HANNAH: Hey! I was wondering if you wanted to go with me to see a movie later. There are some pretty good ones out.

AEGEAN: Oh, shut up!

HANNAH: Excuse me? I'm just politely—

AEGEAN: —I know, Hannah. You can cut the crap now.

HANNAH: *(Nervous.)* Um…what do you mean?

AEGEAN: Jordan told me…he told me everything. I know that he was cheating on me with *you*! I know you two were sneaking around behind my back. Both of you were betraying me. We're best friends, but that obviously means nothing to you. Obviously, you don't care about me at all.

HANNAH: Aegean, you don't understand…

AEGEAN: When were you planning on telling me about all this?

HANNAH: Uh…well…ya see…

AEGEAN: *(Realizing for the first time.)* You weren't going to tell me, were you?

HANNAH: Of course, I was going to tell you!

AEGEAN: Oh yeah? When? After Jordan and I had been going out a year, or what?

HANNAH: How could you possibly be putting all of this on me? You act like Jordan had no part in any of it! You know, you always wished that he was the perfect boyfriend, but he wasn't. You got way too attached to him, and when he rejected you, you couldn't handle it. You can't accept that you aren't—

AEGEAN: —How dare you say that to me. You're actually blaming me for what you did!?

HANNAH: You are so naive. I bet he didn't tell you the rest of the story, did he? He didn't tell you that he wasn't only with me, but there were others. I mean, he and I actually had somewhat of a relationship going...

AEGEAN: *(Sarcastically.)* Yeah, a relationship, while I was his girlfriend. That was probably a really good relationship the two of you had, wasn't it? Sneaking around behind my back, doing God knows what. Real fun, huh?

HANNAH: Aegean, I didn't want this to happen. I didn't want to hurt you.

AEGEAN: You didn't... *(laughing)*...you didn't want to hurt me? Well, guess what, Hannah? You did! I don't know if you expect me to forgive you, or what...

HANNAH: I expect you to have compassion and be a friend.

AEGEAN: And that's what I expected from you, too. But it doesn't always work out like that. You have humiliated, betrayed, and hurt me beyond anything I can express. I can't forgive you. I can't trust you. I never want to see Jordan again and *(beat)* I never want to see you either.

HANNAH: Aegean, please!

AEGEAN: NO! I'm completely disgusted by you, by what you are. I don't even want to look at you. *(On the verge of tears.)* Just...

go back to Jordan. You two, and the rest of his girlfriends, can live happily ever after, without me.

(Hannah hesitates to leave.)

AEGEAN: Hannah, leave!

HANNAH: Right. *(Starts to leave.)* You know, I'll still be here for you, if you ever decide to forgive me. Bye.

(Hannah leaves.)

AEGEAN: *(To herself.)* Forgive her? Yeah right!

MY DAD IS . . .

By Kelly Nish

(Two girls greet one another at the school bus stop.)

AMY: Hey, Amanda, what's wrong?

AMANDA: Nothing.

AMY: No, something's bothering you.

AMANDA: It's my parents.

AMY: What, another fight?

AMANDA: Yeah, but this time my dad left for good.

AMY: Oh my God, I am so sorry.

AMANDA: Thanks.

AMY: But what was the argument about?

AMANDA: My dad's been having an affair.

AMY: Oh, Amanda, I'm really sorry.

AMANDA: Yeah, thanks.

AMY: How long has it been going on?

AMANDA: A couple of months, I think.

AMY: That would explain all the late night trips to the supermarket.

AMANDA: And the business trips to Chicago.

AMY: Wow. I really cannot believe it.

AMANDA: I'm sick of the lies and betrayal.

AMY: So what was her name?

AMANDA: Whose name?

AMY: Your dad's girlfriend!

AMANDA: He didn't have a girlfriend.

AMY: What?

AMANDA: He had a boyfriend...

MOM NEEDS A MAN

By Paige Blatt

(Two girls are relaxing and playing checkers on the front porch of a house.)

ASHLEE: I hate seeing Mom upset. We have to do something about this!

CARY: She doesn't have anyone in her life but us and the bird. That's pretty pathetic.

ASHLEE: I know, but she won't let us help her. Who is there to take her on a date, the grocery man?

CARY: Well, I recently heard that firemen are known to be some of the hottest bachelors around town. So, I was thinking…if you don't mind, I could set you on fire and we'd have to call 911! The firemen would come and mom would fall for at least one of them. I can picture it now…

ASHLEE: Well, you can stop picturing it because there's no chance I am letting you light me on fire. Are you crazy?!

CARY: NO! I happen to think it's a very good idea.

ASHLEE: Well then, why don't I set you on fire?

CARY: I don't think so. Maybe we could set the bird on fire.

ASHLEE: Yeah, but Mom would be so upset about the dead bird. But…there would be a hot fireman to cheer her up!

CARY: Always thinking!

ASHLEE: No, it wouldn't work. I don't want to kill Mr. Squeekers. Can't you go to jail for that? Why don't we stick Mrs. Kinney's cat in the tree?

CARY: You're joking, right? Mrs. Kinney would pull out our teeth before we could even get to the cat.

ASHLEE: Yeah, I know, but it was a nice thought.

(They sit thinking and see a man walk by.)

ASHLEE: Hi, Mr. Swanson! How are you today?

(They look at each other.)

CARY: Mr. Swanson, that's it!

ASHLEE: I don't know how we didn't see it before!

CARY: He's perfect for Mom, and we like him, too.

ASHLEE: Yeah, forget the firemen. We've gotta figure out how to get Mr. Swanson and Mom together.

CARY: But how?

ASHLEE: Follow me…I think I have an idea.

WHAT HAPPENED TO THE NEW GUY?

By Mary Ann Springer

(A girl has witnessed a violent school shooting, and her girlfriend is drilling her for the truth.)

JEAN: Sara, I really want to know what happened in there…can't you tell me? Sara, I'm your best friend; you should be able to tell me what happened. *(Pause.)* Look, I know I can't say that I know what you're going through, because honestly, I don't. Maybe if you just tell me or give me something to go on, I'll have some kind of idea of what you're going through.

SARA: You will never have an idea of what I am going through right now!

JEAN: You're probably right. I won't have any idea because I wasn't there! OK, so tell me why you get *so* emotional when I bring up the new guy who got shot?

SARA: It was *my* fault that he got shot. MY FAULT!

JEAN: How can it be your fault?

SARA: How? I'll tell you how. You know how Tad kept telling everyone he was going to come to school with a gun and shoot anyone who got in his way? He told everyone what time he was going to do it and where, but we all thought he wouldn't do it. I mean, if he was going to do it, why would he tell anyone? We were so wrong.

JEAN: So what does that have to do with the guy who got shot, *the new guy?*

SARA: Well, the day of the shooting, I was flirting with the new guy. And I told him that a boy was going to walk into school that day, threatening people with his gun, and that he was going to shoot people who got in the way of "his plan." But I also told him that Tad wouldn't do anything if someone just stood up to him. Then Tad marched into school and...*(pause)*...BANG! Suddenly, there's Garrett, the new guy, lying on the floor, halfway dead.

JEAN: Oh...my...gosh.

MODELS AND COMEDIANS DON'T MIX

By Mary Ann Springer

(One girl approaches another girl.)

KATIE: *(To herself.)* OK, you are going to tell her that you want to be a comedian. Yes, today will be the day.

HEATHER: Hey! Can you believe Ashlee Simpson at the, um… what color is between red and yellow in the rainbow? Oh, orange! At the Orange Bowl, yeah that's it.

KATIE: I know, I know. That must have been the first time in football history a singer at half time got booed off stage.

HEATHER: Wow, that would be horrible if you got booed off stage. I mean in front of thousands of people, just watching your every move. I would *so* laugh if you, like, got booed off stage at the talent show at school, even though you *are* a really good singer.

KATIE: Yeah, that's good to know. Ummm…I need to tell you something.

HEATHER: OK, what's up?

KATIE: Well, this thing has been on my mind for a long time, and I think it's time I tell you.

HEATHER: Oh my gosh! Are you saying that you have a boyfriend? A boyfriend you haven't told me about?

KATIE: What? No. I want to tell you that I want to be a comedian, like one that stands up.

HEATHER: *(Relieved.)* Oh, thank goodness. A comedian? I am totally going to be a mean girl when I say this, but that is totally social suicide!

KATIE: I think it would be fun.

HEATHER: Hold up. I thought you wanted to be a model, like me, because that is so fetch right now.

KATIE: I think being a comedian would be a lot more fun than being a model, who can't eat anything. But you gotta hear what I have so far, OK?

HEATHER: Sure, OK.

KATIE: You can't laugh right away, OK? *(Pause.)* OK. How's it going? Good? Good. So have you people heard the songs these days? For starters, these songs don't make sense. For example, "You make me wanna lala." OK, Ashlee, what were you doing when you wrote that? OK, and, "You say it best when you say nothing at all." Basically, that song means, SHUT UP! And how about, "The lights are on, but nobody is home." Dude, you're wasting electricity that the state clearly needs, especially the state of California. Yeah. That's it. That's what I got so far.

HEATHER: *(No reaction.)* So, about being a model…

THE THIRD PERSON

By Kelly Nish

(Two girls are sitting together at lunch in the high school cafeteria.)

MONICA: Hey Michelle, guess what?

MICHELLE: You found a pubic hair in your pudding!

MONICA: NO!!

MICHELLE: Well, what?

MONICA: Todd Jacobs asked me to the prom.

MICHELLE: WOW! I thought he only went out with, um, well, you know, popular girls.

MONICA: I know! But I guess all that flirting and waving paid off!

MICHELLE: I guess so! But what are you going to do about Mark?

MONICA: What about him?

MICHELLE: He asked you, too!

MONICA: Oh yeah. I completely forgot about that...

MICHELLE: You better tell him you're going with someone else.

MONICA: I can't do that!

MICHELLE: Why not!?

MONICA: Because it would break his little heart.

MICHELLE: You're right, he's so fragile, you'd think he's gay.

MONICA: I know what I'll do!

MICHELLE: What?

MONICA: I'll tell him that *you* will go with him.

MICHELLE: NO…he's a freak!

MONICA: But you told me he was good boyfriend material.

MICHELLE: I told you that because he was the only one who asked you to the prom. Besides, he talks in the third person! "Mark is going to the movies," or "Mark likes his elective." It creeps me out!

MONICA: Well, I think he's nice, but if you were a real friend, you would do this for me.

MICHELLE: Monica, I better warn you that you will owe me for at least the rest of the school year, maybe even this summer.

MONICA: I will do anything, I promise!

MICHELLE: OK, fine.

MONICA: You're the best, Michelle!

MICHELLE: We'll see.

DIET CRAZE

By Kelly Nish

(Two girls are walking together between classes.)

MADISON: What would you say if I told you I was going on a diet?

KELSEY: I would say you were crazy! You don't need to lose weight!

MADISON: Josh Evans seems to think so.

KELSEY: What? What did he say?

MADISON: Well, it started when I asked him if he was busy Friday night, and he said, "Are you asking me out?" and I said, "Sort of," then...

KELSEY: What Maddy? You can tell me. What did he say?

MADISON: He said, "I don't go out with anyone who weighs more than I do."

KELSEY: Are you serious? You know he is such a self-centered jerk! He doesn't think about anyone but himself!

MADISON: Do you think if I lost fifteen pounds, he would go out with me?

KELSEY: MADISON!! You can't let his stupid comments affect you this much.

MADISON: But I really do want to lose some weight.

KELSEY: Are you sure? If you go on a diet, you have to promise me that you are doing it for yourself and nobody else.

MADISON: I'm sure! When Josh asks me out, once I am skinny, I'll say, "NO, you had your chance."

KELSEY: That's the Madison I know! So, this diet, it can't be easy, so you're going to need some moral support.

MADISON: And…

KELSEY: I'll do it with you.

MADISON: Really?

KELSEY: Yeah.

MADISON: Kelsey, that means sooooo much to me!!!

KELSEY: I'm glad.

MADISON: So, a diet. How do we start?

KELSEY: I don't know. Let's ask my sister, she's always dieting for boys.

MADISON: If we loose weight by the end of the week, do you think I'll be over Josh by then?

KELSEY: I think you already are. Come on, let's go!

JUST FRIENDS

By Samantha Grossman

(Two sisters are communicating in their bedroom's vanity mirror.)

KATIE: Isn't that Mom's lipstick you're wearing?

KENDALL: If you're looking to tattle, don't bother. She offered it to me.

KATIE: *(Beat.)* So…when is he coming to pick you up?

KENDALL: Who?

KATIE: Your date! What's his name?

KENDALL: Oh, you mean Billy.

KATIE: Yeah, Billy.

KENDALL: I'm meeting him at the In-N-Out Burger at six, and then we're going to walk over to the theater.

KATIE: Isn't that a bit unromantic?

KENDALL: Well, if you must know, we're really just going as friends. Besides, what do you know about being romantic? You're eleven! *(Giggle.)*

KATIE: I'll be twelve in three months, and then you'll only be four years older. Anyway, I know plenty! Mom lets me watch PG-13 movies, remember?

KENDALL: And this is just like in the movies, too. Girl meets boy, boy asks girl to go steady, and girl says YES!

KATIE: So you do like him!?

KENDALL: Of course I do. Why else would I agree to torture myself at a greasy, disgusting burger joint if I didn't?

KATIE: Then Billy thinks you're going as friends, and you really like him, but don't want to let on that you do. Isn't this always the same situation we girls find our vulnerable selves in when we fall too hard for the wrong guy?

KENDALL: That's it, Carrie Bradshaw! Out! This is only my very first date and I'm not about to let my pint-sized baby sister psyche me out.

KATIE: Carrie who? OK, OK…but before I go, can you find out if he has a younger brother?

KENDALL: Out with you, you PG-13-movie-watching fiend!

GUYS DON'T LISTEN

By Tess Christiansen

(Two girls are talking.)

KIM: Oh my God, did I tell you?

JENNA: What…tell me what?

KIM: James thinks I like him!

JENNA: James…Dobson?

KIM: Yeah.

JENNA: Why does he think you like him? Do you?

KIM: No, I don't! But, like, he thinks I like him because I go to all the baseball games, and he's on the team, and I yell and root for him, but only because we're friends. He thinks I go to the games just to watch him.

JENNA: And that's it? He thinks you like him because you go to the baseball games?

KIM: Yeah, that, and…once I was talking to Cameron, who's also on the team, and I was joking around with him and said that I was in love with James and that I wanted to go out with him. But I thought he knew I was joking, because we were laughing and stuff.

JENNA: Well, did he tell James?

KIM: Yeah, he did. But not only James…he told, like, everyone on the team, and now they're all making fun of me.

JENNA: God! Why did Cameron have to go and be so stupid?

KIM: I don't know, but he's always being queer like that.

JENNA: Yeah, that's true.

KIM: And no matter how many times I tell all of them that I don't like James and that I was just joking, they never listen!

JENNA: Do guys ever listen? Maybe they want you to like James because he likes you.

KIM: I don't think so. But it sucks now, because James thinks I like him, so he doesn't hang around with us at lunch anymore, and he never talks to me, and he, like, avoids looking at me.

JENNA: Oh man, that stinks. You got rejected by a guy you don't even like! That's pretty sad.

(They both laugh.)

KIM: I know! Don't laugh at me!

JENNA: I'm sorry, but it is pretty funny.

KIM: It's totally self-centered of him to think that I go to the games just for him. It's like, dude, come on, you aren't the only person I know on the team. And I don't cheer just for him...I cheer for everyone.

JENNA: Yeah, but he only hears it when you're yelling for him. Do you want me to talk to him about it? I could tell him that he isn't the only guy in the world, and that you two are just friends, and not to assume such crazy things...of course, saying all that without hurting his ego too much.

KIM: *(Laughing.)* Thanks, Jenna...but I'll just talk to him myself. Maybe.

(They both laugh.)

JENNA: Guys!

SATURDAY NIGHT

By Amber Gonzales

(One girl enters the room, upset. The other girl is sitting, waiting for her.)

BRITTANY: So what did she say?

SARAH: She said no.

BRITTANY: WHAT? WHY?

SARAH: She doesn't want me out that late at night…whatever! She lets my sister do anything she wants.

BRITTANY: You should bring that up.

SARAH: I did.

BRITTANY: And what did she say to that?

SARAH: "Yes Sarah, but Amy is older than you."

BRITTANY: Oh, come on! By a year!

SARAH: I KNOW!! And she still let her do whatever she wanted when *she* was 17!

BRITTANY: I'm sorry, but that really sucks.

SARAH: Yeah, well, when I turn 18 this summer, I'm gonna do whatever I want, and nothing's gonna stop me. I just don't see why she doesn't trust me. Your parents trust you, right?

BRITTANY: Yeah, and I mean, it's not like you're a bad kid or anything.

SARAH: Yeah, I'm a good kid…I'm a good *YOUNG ADULT!*

BRITTANY: YES! A very good young adult…who…gets good grades.

SARAH: The honor roll!

BRITTANY: You're never late to class…ever.

SARAH: Not once!

BRITTANY: And you always do your chores.

SARAH: I know! I'm, like, so disgustingly responsible!

BRITTANY: Well your room's never clean, but hey! No one's perfect…

SARAH: Yeah, that's true.

BRITTANY: BUT, you're always going out of your way to help others. And you never give in to peer pressure!

SARAH: Yeah…YEAH! And you know what else? I have never touched a drug or alcoholic beverage in my life!

BRITTANY: Yeah, we just don't do that.

SARAH: WE DON'T! WE never lie, cheat, or steal. WE are strong, mature, independent young women!

BRITTANY: AMEN, SISTER!

SARAH: And all I'm asking for is a little trust and a little freedom!

BRITTANY: YEAH!

SARAH: I'm tired of sitting around here every single Saturday night, watching the same movies and eating junk food! I want to go out and have FUN!

BRITTANY: So what are you going to do about it?

SARAH: I'll tell you what I'm gonna do about it! Yeah! I'm gonna walk back down those stairs and tell my mother exactly how I feel! I'm going to walk right up to her and say, "Mother, I must speak with you. I am no longer a child, and I deserve to be treated like the adult I am."

BRITTANY: OK…you do that!

SARAH: Oh, what!? You don't believe me?

BRITTANY: Well, no…

SARAH: Well, I will! Yeah, I'm going right now!

(Sarah exits room, then enters again a few seconds later.)

SARAH: Tomorrow…. She's kind of busy right now. I just don't want to bother her.

BRITTANY: Uh huh, yeah…whatever. So what do you want to do? Watch a movie, perhaps?

SARAH: Sure…let's see what choices we have this time…

BRITTANY: I'm guessing, SAME AS LAST TIME!

SARAH: *(Sarcastically.)* Good one.

BRITTANY: Why don't we just go rent a new one?

SARAH: Got any money?

BRITTANY: No.

SARAH: Me either, so we're stuck with these.

BRITTANY: NO!! I'm not watching another Disney movie! If I have to watch Bambi's mom die one more time…!

SARAH: OK!

BRITTANY: And we're not watching *Sleepless in Seattle*.

SARAH: OH…come on! The Disney thing I can understand, but *Sleepless in Seattle* is AMAZING!

BRITTANY: We've watched it a thousand times!

SARAH: BECAUSE IT'S AMAZING!

BRITTANY: NO! God, just go talk to your mom!

SARAH: No, no!

BRITTANY: WHY NOT? SHES YOUR MOTHER! You live with her! Are you afraid of your own mother?

SARAH: No…but I know she'll never listen.

BRITTANY: Just GO!

SARAH: Fine. I know you'll never let me relax unless I go…so I'll go.

BRITTANY: You'll go *now.*

SARAH: OK, I'll go now…. I'm going, MOTHER!

(Sarah exits the room, and puts on a fake mother's voice. Brittany listens in disbelief.)

SARAH: MOM!

FAKE MOM VOICE: Yes, honey?

SARAH: I need to talk to you. Brittany and I wanted to go out with some friends tonight, and we were thinking, because we're adults now, that it would be OK.

FAKE MOM VOICE: Oh yes, I know, of course you can go. You're strong, mature, and independent young women, and you've got really great style!

SARAH: Thanks, mom. Love ya!

(Sarah comes back in the room to find Brittany right at the door.)

SARAH: Hey, Brittany…she said yes.

BRITTANY: No, she didn't. You amaze me. You actually thought I'd believe that load of crap!

SARAH: Well…

BRITTANY: This is ridiculous. Sit down!

(Brittany forces Sarah into a chair.)

BRITTANY: Look at me. How do you live with yourself! You're a COWARD. You can't even ask your own mother to go out on a Saturday night! How do you expect to make it through life!?

SARAH: Cautiously…

BRITTANY: Cautiously?

SARAH: Cautiously and safely.

BRITTANY: Ohmigod, fine. *I'll* go talk to your mom.

SARAH: Are you serious?

BRITTANY: Yes!

SARAH: Wait…no really? Are you serious?

(Brittany exits. Sarah sits looking nervous.)

Scenes for Two Boys

BEST FRIENDS

By Tess Christiansen

(Two boys are talking in a gym.)

KEN: Hey dude, what's goin' on?

BILL: Uh…hi. *(Nervous.)* Um…Ken…look, I gotta talk to you about something.

KEN: Yeah, OK. Go ahead.

BILL: OK, I gotta talk to you about your problem.

KEN: What? Yeah, I guess I do too much homework. I can take a break right now. What game do you want to play?

BILL: No, actually, I was talking about your problem with… bulimia.

KEN: What?! Bulimia?! Listen dude, I am 17 and on the cross-country team. Why would someone need to be bulimic? Jeez, Bill, do you think I'm a chick or something?

BILL: No, I don't, but Ken, I know you have a problem. I'm pretty sure your mom knows, and I think you know it, too.

KEN: So what makes you think this Bill? Huh? What makes you think I am bulimic?

BILL: Well, I see you, or hear you, throwing up a lot.

KEN: Yeah, well, I get sick like anyone else. You know that. I get flus and viruses and eat bad cafeteria food! Sometimes I throw it up.

BILL: No, Ken, you purposely throw it up. After your chocolate, your chips, your soda. You do it because you have to keep your weight down for the cross-country team.

KEN: Why are you saying these things to me?

BILL: You need to stop denying it. You have an eating disorder.

KEN: NO, I DON'T!

BILL: It's a serious problem that I want to help you with, and I am sure your mom would want to help you, too.

KEN: OH YEAH? And what would my dad say about all this? He'd think I can't even control myself, that I'm like some dumb teenage girl, and that I'm not a real athlete!

BILL: No one would have to tell your dad. It could just be the three of us.

KEN: NO!

BILL: Ken, why don't you understand? You have to stop! You're *killing* yourself!!

KEN: I think you should leave now, Bill. It's 9:00 and my dad doesn't like people over past 9:30.

BILL: Come on, Ken. Now it's your time to take control of your own life.

(Ken shrugs and Bill walks out.)

BET ON LOVE

By Tess Christiansen

(Two boys are playing video games in a bedroom and are later joined by a girl.)

PRESTON: Do you think Franky's cute?

TOBEY: Ewww. Why would you ask me that? She's my best friend. I don't see her as a girl…she's more like a very feminine-looking gay guy, but not a girl.

PRESTON: Oh come on! So you're telling me that you never. . .checked her out or anything?

TOBEY: Uh, not that I can remember.

PRESTON: Not even before you guys became good friends?

TOBEY: I don't know.

PRESTON: Well, I don't know how you couldn't. I mean, I see her as a guy most of the time, too, but she's still hot.

TOBEY: When was the last time you heard me say a girl was "hot"?

PRESTON: Yeah, you're right.

TOBEY: Can you pass me my soda?

PRESTON: Yeah, sure. Are you certain that you don't find Franky attractive at all? 'Cause we kinda have a bet going.

TOBEY: What kind of bet!?

PRESTON: Just that in the next six months, you and Franky are going to end up boyfriend and girlfriend.

TOBEY: Really!?

PRESTON: Well, yeah. I mean, everyone is always saying that you two should be going out, or that you'll get married when you're older. We just thought we'd put some money on it.

TOBEY: I don't know. I never really looked at her in that way. Did she say something about liking me?

PRESTON: No...do you think she does!?

TOBEY: Not really, but people used to say that a lot. And, she told me that she used to think I was hot. I dunno, I guess she is...

(Franky walks in on the boys talking.)

FRANKY: Hey guys! What are you doing?

(Silence.)

FRANKY: Are you guys OK? I wasn't interrupting some kind of weird guy ritual, was I? *(Pause.)* Right...OK. Well, I'm gonna go the bathroom. I'll be right back.

(She leaves.)

PRESTON: Whoa. Crazy timing she has, huh? Jeez. I think she might suspect we were talking about her.

TOBEY: Or that we're doing drugs...

PRESTON: *(Laughing.)* What were you going to say before she came in?

TOBEY: Nothing, I wasn't gonna say anything.

PRESTON: Yes you were! Were you about to say that you've secretly been in love with her this whole time and you're finally going to express your love for her?

TOBEY: Hardly! I think I was about to tell you to shut up. I hate it when people talk about me and Franky, because it will never happen.

(Franky comes back in.)

FRANKY: OK, so have you guys stopped smoking the crack cocaine, and gone back to acting like regular guys again?

TOBEY: Oh come on, we weren't doin' drugs. We were just talking.

FRANKY: *(Laughing.)* You guys were talking? About what?

TOBEY/PRESTON: NOTHING!

FRANKY: All right!

PRESTON: You know, Franky, Tobey has something he wants to tell you.

TOBEY: No I don't!

PRESTON: Oh, sure you do. Come on, now's your chance.

FRANKY: What are guys talking about? Tell me!

PRESTON: Can I tell her?

TOBEY: NO! Just stop! They're isn't *anything* to tell!

PRESTON: OK, fine. Calm down.

FRANKY: Whoa, that was weird. All right, so getting back to what's actually going on…did you guys want to get something to eat?

PRESTON: Yeah, I'll go.

TOBEY: I'm just gonna stay home.

FRANKY: Fine. I'll meet you downstairs, Preston.

PRESTON: OK.

(Franky leaves.)

PRESTON: Dude, if you really are in love with her, just tell her. Stop acting so weird. It's OK if you are. People will be shocked at first, but the name-calling will ease after a few months.

TOBEY: But, I... ohhh...I don't know.

PRESTON: Right. OK, we'll see you later then.

(Preston leaves.)

TOBEY: *(To himself.)* Like her? *(Pause.)* No way.

<u>Scenes for a Boy and a Girl</u>

AT LEAST I'VE GOT A DATE

By Tess Christiansen

(A boy and girl are chatting.)

MARTY: So, are you coming over tomorrow?

CELIA: No, I've got a date.

MARTY: A date? Why?

CELIA: What do you mean, why? Don't you mean to say, with whom?

MARTY: No, I mean, why are you going out on a date?

CELIA: How rude! I'm going out on a date because I was asked and I accepted.

MARTY: Who is it?

CELIA: Mel Millings.

MARTY: *(Sarcastically.)* Oh, cool.

(Moment of silence.)

MARTY: Oh, come on! Mel Millings! Are you serious? The guy has three lip piercings, they're always infected, and it looks like he has a raging case of herpes.

CELIA: He does not have herpes…I don't think. He's cool.

MARTY: Oh please, he's only trying to steal your candy.

CELIA: Oh, yeah, 'cause you know a whole lot about that subject! At least I've *got* a date. Who are you going to be spending this Friday night with? Master Chief?

MARTY: Hey! Do not make fun of Master Chief!

CELIA: OK, whatever.

MARTY: You're stupid. I could have a date if I wanted. There are tons of girls who would go out with me.

CELIA: Yeah, the only problem is that they aren't men. *(Laughing.)*

MARTY: You know, I don't really mind all the gay jokes, but when you say it around other people, they start thinking it's actually true.

CELIA: What the heck? Who thought that?

MARTY: Deborah. I guess she heard you and Travis talking in class or something. She went and told Cassandra that I was gay.

CELIA: She is so idiotic, I just want to punch her!

MARTY: Wait! We are not done talking about your date.

CELIA: Yeah, I think we're done. I heard what you had to say.

MARTY: No, you haven't. I have something to ask you. Can I go on the date with you?

CELIA: Um…do you mean like a double date? Is there a guy you'd like to go on a date with?

MARTY: Uh, no. It's a girl, thank you very much, butt face! I want Cassandra to go.

CELIA: You...and...Cassandra? Really? Did you suddenly go into an alternate reality where she was never your girlfriend and she and I never hated each other?

MARTY: No, I'm completely aware of those things. So is it OK?

CELIA: You're such a dork! *(Pause.)* OK, you know what...sure, why not? We're going to be at the pizza place around 7:30. God, this should be interesting.

(Celia walks off stage.)

MARTY: Oh, you have no idea. *(Cunning smile.)*

JACKY and CHAD

By Monique Almanza

(A boy and girl run into each other, standing in line to buy concert tickets.)

JACKY: Hey…what's up? I haven't talked to *you* in awhile.

CHAD: Nothin' much. Boy, it feels weird talking to you again. Don't ask why…it's just a feeling that I can't explain.

JACKY: Yeah, I know how you feel.

CHAD: You did stupid things to me back then…but I have a life now. I can't keep going and looking for the little things, like our relationship.

JACKY: Our relationship was NOT little! At least not for me. I really thought it was something special.

CHAD: Yeah, well everyone thinks differently and I need to get going. My friends are waiting for me.

JACKY: Wow, I totally forgot we were supposed to be at a party. Boy, time passes by fast when you get in a good conversation, huh?

CHAD: This was not a conversation. It was something that should have never happened. Don't worry, because it won't happen again.

JACKY: Look, I am sorry for doing all those terrible things to you when we were going out. I thought that…I don't know what I thought, but I do know that I liked you and still do.

CHAD: Well, you might be sorry, but what you did, it's already passed and you can't change the past. OK, well... bye.

JACKY: Wait!

CHAD: What! What do you want to know, Jacky? What do you want from me? What we had is over and done! There's nothing that is going to change that! Nothing!! So get over it!

JACKY: Chad!! I never thought of you—

CHAD: —me, what? What were you going to say, Jacky...that I fell for all those lies you told me? That I'm a loser for going out with you, like every other guy you went out with!?

JACKY: NO! Not at all! Chad, you got it all wrong! I wasn't going to say that! I was just going to say that I'm sorry. I am sorry. I didn't want to hurt you the way I did. I never wanted to hurt you in the first place. You meant, and mean, so much to me.

CHAD: Well, guess what? You hurt me!! No one will ever hurt me like you did. And I won't let it happen again. I'll make sure of it.

JACKY: You know something, I thought that you would be different, but I guess I was wrong. I understand if you don't want to talk to me again, but I want you to know that I still care about you, even if you are mad at me.

(Jacky goes offstage.)

CHAD: *(To himself.)* How did things end up like this? I still like you too, Jacky, but you hurt me too much. Bye, Jacky.

THE FIGHT

By Chelsea Matthews

(A boy and girl are arguing.)

MICHAEL: Alex, wait! I'm sorry! Can we please just talk about this!?

ALEX: Fine! You want to talk? Let's talk about how you betrayed me for Sarah, of all people! How could you do that to me?

MICHAEL: I'm sorry. I didn't mean to. It…just…happened, and besides, *she* kissed me!

ALEX: Oh yeah! And you put up a HUGE fight, didn't you! Will you just leave me alone? You're nothing but trouble anyway.

MICHAEL: What do I have to do to make you believe me?!

ALEX: NOTHING! There's nothing you can do, because you've already done the worst.

MICHAEL: You know, you're not being fair about this at all!

ALEX: FAIR! You want to talk about what's not fair? You lying to me and kissing my best friend isn't fair either, Michael! You think that makes me feel good, hearing the whole school talk about how *my* boyfriend kissed my best friend! Is that fair?

MICHAEL: Well, do you think I felt good when you cheated on me with John?

ALEX: That was a long time ago, and besides, that was just a rumor! Wait a second, is this pay back for John?

MICHAEL: NO!!!!! I'm telling you how I felt when it happened!!

ALEX: No, you're not! You're trying to pay me back for that stupid rumor, aren't you? Just forget it, and go back to Sarah!

MICHAEL: Why don't you believe me? You act like this was all my fault, as if Sarah had nothing to do with this.

ALEX: Don't turn this around on me! You're the one who lied and went behind my back. How could I ever believe someone who lied to me like that? Let me ask you one thing. Why Sarah? She's my best friend! I mean…what does she have that I don't?

MICHAEL: Look, Alex. It was something that should have never happened, but it did, and I'm REALLY sorry for it. Can you please believe me when I say, I didn't mean it?

ALEX: I don't know, at least not right now. It's too much to think about right now.

MICHAEL: Just give me one more chance…please?

ALEX: I'll think about it, but I am not promising anything!

MICHAEL: Fine.

(Alex starts to walk away.)

MICHAEL: Alex?

ALEX: Yeah?

MICHAEL: I just wanted to say…thanks.

(Alex smiles as she walks away.)

GEEKS AND JOCKS

By Kelly Nish

(A boy rushes to his female friend for advice.)

LEO: Jenna, I need your help.

JENNA: Sure, but you don't want me to beat someone up for you again, do you?

LEO: No, it's Alexa.

JENNA: You don't want me to beat her up, do you? Because after that last incident, we're friends now.

LEO: I want to ask her to the dance. But I don't really know how to approach her, talk to her, or actually be with her.

JENNA: So in other words, you've never spoken to her.

LEO: No. In first grade we carpooled.

JENNA: Listen, Leo. It's an unwritten rule that cheerleaders go to the dances with the football players. They don't go with the A/V crew, chess players, or the guys in the science club.

LEO: But this could be my chance to change those rules. Besides, science can be really cool.

JENNA: Leo, let's get back to reality.

LEO: Yeah, the reality is, she's HOT! Her eyes are so blue and her hair is so blonde...she's so HOT!

JENNA: HEL-LO!?

LEO: Hi? *(Confused.)*

JENNA: Look, maybe it would be better if you two were just friends.

LEO: Just friends? Just friends with the woman of my dreams?

JENNA: Woman of your dreams? What does she have that I don't...I mean, that other girls don't?

LEO: Other girls? What other girls would I want?

JENNA: I'll talk to her for you.

LEO: OK, but make sure you tell her that I don't need those glasses...I can wear contacts.

JENNA: Leo, we've lived next door to each other all our lives, we used to play football together, heck, we even played dress up. Trust me, I know you.

LEO: Thanks Jenna, you're a good friend.

(Leo starts to leave.)

JENNA: *(To herself.)* He looks right past me. Yeah, I'm a jock, but he's a science geek. We're equally unpopular. I'd go to the dance with him, if only he'd ask. I just don't get it.

LEO: *(To himself.)* What am I thinking? I should be asking Jenna to the dance. But what if she said no? Who am I kidding...we're just friends.

MONEY RULES

By Lee C. Korelitz

(A boy is pacing behind his sister, reciting lines with passion, while she is sitting on the couch, looking rather annoyed at his pathetic attempt.)

LENNY: "AND BY THE HOLY MIGHTY OF GOD! I shall sanctify this hellish place. In the name of the holiest of holy gods, by smiting ye down to hell with the holy holly from high in the hills of Hillsbrad. Hark hellish unholy beast for the HOLY WRATH OF—"

JENNIFER: —HOLY CRAP! Lenny, shut the hell up!

LENNY: *(Mumbling.)* Unholy hell…no, that's not it. Unholy… Damn it, Jennifer! You made me lose my line.

JENNIFER: It's a sign from the divine, telling you that you need to give it a damn break.

LENNY: But I need to get this role.

JENNIFER: This script sucks, bro.

LENNY: But the paycheck doesn't. Now, if you'll let me continue. I will continue to practice, so I can get that damn part and get a helluva lot of money in the process.

JENNIFER: This script is absolutely terrible. The most anyone should get paid is a free meal and the hope that the immortal soul won't be cast down to hell for performing this abomination.

LENNY: $12.3 million, sis.

JENNIFER: WHAT?

LENNY: It pays $12.3 million. My manager told me today. But, I guess you're right. I am not really the one to sacrifice dignity for money.

JENNIFER: Forget about your dignity! That's $12.3 freaking million.

LENNY: So...it's just money.

JENNIFER: Think about what you can buy with that kind of money! THINK!

LENNY: World peace?

JENNIFER: Let the world blow itself to hell and back for all you care, because you can buy a brand spanking new—

LENNY: —BED!

JENNIFER: Whatever! You buy the mansion to put your bed in first and a few cars to put in the 3000-foot garage.

LENNY: *(Excited.)* Yeah, with razor sharp barbed wire for keeping out that evil man who keeps walking his dog to *our* yard. No wait...LANDMINES!

JENNIFER: Landmines, I like. And a boat...you need a boat.

LENNY: And a big screen TV.

JENNIFER: AND MONKEYS?!

LENNY: Monkeys?

JENNIFER: Think about it for a second...monkeys.

LENNY: *(He gets it slowly.)* Yeah...monkeys.

JENNIFER: Now go back to practicing, so you can nail this audition and buy me a new computer.

LENNY: YES! All right, time to go back to practice so I can buy everything we want!

JENNIFER: Go get em' tiger! One ride to the audition is at least fifty dollars in gas. The new mansion will be around $3 million. Putting me in the will, and Lenny having a terrible, costly accident…priceless.

FAMILY TV TALK

By David Phillips

(A female tutor and a young boy are sitting at a desk. The kid has his arms crossed, obviously not enjoying himself. The tutor is frustrated. Later they are joined by the boy's sister, her boyfriend, and then the older sister.)

T: Twelve divided by seven does not equal UPN! Never mind. OK, fine, kid.

MJF: Michaeljfox.

T: OK, Michael.

MJF: Uh-uh. Michaeljfox.

T: Fine. Michaeljfox. Let's just move on to analogies. (*Flips through book.*) Ladder is to stepping as street is to…?

MJF: *The Fairly OddParents* episode where they were babysat by Grandpa, and all modern stuff was bunk, and Timmy Turner asked his fairy godparents why everything was the 1930s…

T: No, you're not understanding the problem. Let's try this again. OK. Legs are to pants as chest is…?

MJF: *That's So Raven*, when Raven's team needed a $100 calculator and instead bought—

T: —No! Not even close! The answer is one word, give me one word. One. OK…3 is to triangle is as 4 is to…

MJF: SpongeBob!

T: It's square. Square!

MJF: I said that!

T: No, you didn't! You didn't even try! You're completely off base. Your mother is going to freak!

(*Marytylermoore pops her head in from the bedroom door.*)

MTM: Could you mute, please?

T: I'm sorry! I'm sorry, it's just that your brother, here, is not getting his homework! I don't know where he's getting this stuff!

MTM: (*Surprised.*) Really? (*Turns to brother.*) Ryan on *The OC* is to Trey as Batman is…?

MJF: Batman is to the Joker.

MTM: Exactly!

MJF: I know!

MTM: (*Stares at the tutor, confused.*) Seems fine to me.

T: No, you see, that…that's not going to be on the test. Like, any test, ever. Maybe a *TV Guide* questionnaire, but…

(*Enter the boyfriend. He's a cool snowboarder type.*)

B: (*Like the Fonz.*) Heyyyyy.

MTM: Oh! (*To the tutor.*) This is the Sayid to my Shannon. The Seth to my Summer. The Clark to my Lana.

T: …Your boyfriend.

B: Hey babe, you're going overkill, like on EXPN when Jamie Bestwick pulls a double tailwhip flair.

MTM: Sorry.

B: What's the score in tonight's game?

MTM: They were having a Ryan-not-knowing-he-should-study-architecture moment.

B: I'd like to study you! I'd like to study you the way the X Games does instant replay on Antti Autti's superpipe backside nine.

(*MTM slaps the boyfriend's arm coyly.*)

MJF: Ewww! Marytylermoore is getting TV-MA in my room!!!

T: What is wrong with all of you people???

(*The tutor slams the book and tries to grab her backpack, but the boyfriend is sitting on it. She tries to pull it out from under him.*)

MTM: I love you more than on *Desperate Housewives* when Susan, AKA Teri Hatcher, loves Mike, AKA James Denton.

B: I want you more than Mankind wants a Heavyweight Championship belt.

MTM: I need you more than Haley needs Nathan on *One Tree Hill,* when Haley was on tour, even after she annulled but didn't annul the marriage.

B: I'll take you like Big Show takes on Triple H *on WWE Smackdown!*

(*Oprahwinfrey barges into the doorway, and MJF stands behind her, all cocky.*)

OW: What's going on here?

T: Oh, thank God! I was trying to tutor and then they started getting—

MTM: —Ohmigod, Haley was Nathan's tutor!

OW: I can handle this. Michaeljfox, cover your ears. (*He does so. To MTM...*) Marytylermoore, if you don't leave this room like

Marissa's dad leaves in *The OC*, I will take you down like Big Pussy in *The Sopranos'* season 2 finale. (*To the boyfriend who find this really hot...*) And as for you, I'll cut you open like the masked murder does in *Nip/Tuck,* and then I'm gonna lose it like Chiklis on *The Shield.* You'll be begging for the commish from me, but like Avon from *The Wire,* you'll know it's not gonna stop. You're *Deadwood,* you hear me? I will *Curb Your Enthusiasm* so bad, you'll wish you were *Six Feet Under.* There will be no *Angels in America* for you! (*She looks behind herself to make sure it's safe.*) You're going down like Cary Elwes from *Saw 2.*

B: Wow.

MTM: Movie reference! (*MTM runs out of the room crying. The boyfriend runs after her. He keeps staring at the older sister. The boyfriend runs into the wall because of it. OW smiles and walks out. MJF looks at T.*)

T: I think we're done now. I'm gonna go home and destroy my TiVo.

TECH SUPPORT

By David Phillips

(College computer lab. A young lady is sitting at a desk with a sign that reads "Tech Support." She's reading Wittgenstein. A young man comes in with computer in case. He looks around and sees the sign, then walks up. She doesn't look up.)

TIM: Um, it's Audrey, right? We were both in Swig dorm last year, not on the same flat.

AUDREY: *(Looks up.)* Flat? Are you serious? Fine, can I help you?

TIM: *(Confused.)* My…computer has a file and I've somehow misplaced it, and I was wondering if you could find it for me.

AUDREY: I'm afraid I can't.

TIM: But you're tech support. Isn't this your job?

AUDREY: What bachelors program are you in?

TIM: Well, I'm an English major, but my focus is—

AUDREY: —That's very close to what I asked for. I am sorry, but this table has an intelligence quotient, and I'm afraid you don't quite make it.

TIM: Are *you* serious?

AUDREY: It's quite the pickle you are in. I'm sure they'll be able to help you. *(She points away and then looks back at her book. He turns and starts to walk in that direction and then stops. There's no one else. He returns to the desk.)*

TIM: I'm not entirely sure how to deal with this melee, here. I'm sorry, I feel as if I've perturbed you in some fashion. I'm Tim.

AUDREY: I know. You lived on a nearby "flat." And you didn't use "perturbed" correctly.

TIM: Indeed. But you knew what I meant.

AUDREY: I really can't help you, but you would have better luck asking Smarmy Jim.

TIM: The janitor with the teeth thing?

AUDREY: Yes, Smarmy Jim, the janitor with the teeth thing.

TIM: Look, I just need one file off of this bloody computer.

AUDREY: You really shouldn't use English colloquialisms if you're not English.

TIM: It's one file.

AUDREY: I highly recommend it, though.

TIM: You recommend the file?

AUDREY: I recommend England. I'm not really part of your conversation…I'm accidentally in front of you.

TIM: It'll take you less than five minutes.

AUDREY: I genuinely can't. We're not supposed to deal with immigrant computers.

TIM: Please help me find the file…it's one file!

AUDREY: What is the file?

TIM: It's a paper for class.

AUDREY: What's in the file?

TIM: A novella.

AUDREY: What's it about?

TIM: I'm not gonna tell you!

AUDREY: What's the title?

TIM: *Iris.*

AUDREY: That's a terrible name.

TIM: Excuse me?

AUDREY: I'm kidding. All right, let's have a look-see.

TIM: All right.

AUDREY: What the…!

TIM: Is there a problem? Did you break it…?

AUDREY: The file's right here.

TIM: Oh yeah, I know…

AUDREY: It's the only thing on the desktop.

TIM: I sort of just needed a way to say hi…

AUDREY: You didn't need me to help you *at all?*

TIM: Yes, this is me hitting—

AUDREY: —Are you hitting on me?

TIM: Awkwardly, but yes.

AUDREY: This is how you pick up girls?

TIM: I was going to walk up and kiss you, but this seemed more feasible.

AUDREY: Or complicated!

TIM: Turned out that way.

AUDREY: We know why you don't date much.

TIM: So, it didn't work?

AUDREY: I didn't say that.

TIM: Good, 'cause—

AUDREY: —If you had just kissed me, you'd be much further ahead in the game.

TIM: Isn't that a little forward?

AUDREY: Can be, but not necessarily.

(*He leans in to kiss her. She leans back. He realizes...*)

TIM: No panache, huh?

AUDREY: No panache.

TIM: I will return.

AUDREY: Bring a better pick up line.

TIM: I will return prepared. (*He smiles and leaves.*)

AUDREY: Good, because I don't want to wait any longer to kiss you than I have.

Order Form

To order copies of *Scenes for Teens by Teens* you can:

Order by phone: 1-818-523-8283

Order online at: www.DianeChristiansen.com

Postal order: 26532 Bighorn Way, Valencia, Ca, 91354

Please send ____ copies of *Scenes for Teens by Teens* by Diane Christiansen

Name: _____

Address: _____

City: _____ State: _____
Zip:_____

Telephone: _____

Email address: _____

Shipping: $4.50 for the first book

        $1.00 for each additional book

Cost per copy: $14.95

Sub Total: _____

Total: _____

Please make checks payable to: Diane Christiansen